Dancing Down the Hallway

SPIRITUAL
REFLECTIONS
FOR THE
EVERY DAY

Dancing Down the Hallway

Kelly A. Fryer
Timothy J. Ressmeyer

Augsburg
MINNEAPOLIS

DANCING DOWN THE HALLWAY
Spiritual Reflections for the Every Day

Cover and interior design by David Meyer.
Illustrations by Kelly A. Fryer.

ISBN 0-8066-4432-X

The paper used in this publication meets the minimum requirements of American National Standard for Information Sciences—Permanence of Paper for Printed Library Materials, ANSI Z329.48-1984.

Printed in Canada

05   04   03   02   01   1   2   3   4   5   6   7   8   9   10

"We love because God first loved us."

1 JOHN 4:19

Contents

Introduction

Have you ever wondered what people get out of reading the Bible? Does starting at "page one" and working your way through it seem like an overwhelming challenge? Are you a little skeptical that there is even anything worth reading in there? Then this book might be just what you need to begin falling in love with God's word.

The Word of God is alive and full of good news for you. Let it surprise you. Let it sing to you. Let it speak to you and change you and challenge you and help you know you're not alone.

Our hope is that what you experience here will open you up to the reality of a God who is always with you, in the darkness and in the daylight, in your sorrow and in your joy. We are hoping that you will meet here a God who wants to take you by the hand and dance with you . . . right down the middle of your every day.

Have fun.

One

*Let us eat and celebrate; for this child
of mine was dead and is alive again;
was lost and now is found!"*

FROM LUKE 15:23-24

Nobody is ever so
Lost
That God can't
Find
Them.

Everybody
Gets
Lost
Sometimes.

- Think back five years. Were you lost? Or Found?

- What was the reason behind your last celebration?

- Where do you go when you don't want anyone to find you?

- Who do you know who is in need of a welcoming?

- What is that dog on the "lost dog" poster on the telephone pole feeling right now?

Two

God shows love to us in this way:
God's Son was sent into the world.

FROM 1 JOHN 9

The boy put down
his crayon.
"Dad,
do you love me?"
"Of course I do,
silly.
You know that."

"I know," he said
with a grin.
"Sometimes a kid
just needs to hear it."
And he went back
To coloring in
The sky.

- Why did you last say, "I love you"?

- Who loves you even when you're unlovable?

- Where does the sky end?

- When you stop—what do you think about?

- What was the last thing that made you smile?

Three

*"Now the Lord came and stood there, calling as before,
'Samuel! Samuel!' And Samuel said, 'Speak, for
your servant is listening.'"*

1 SAMUEL 3:10

He was humming
A tune
I didn't recognize
And dancing
Down
The
Hallway.

He must have heard
A song
I couldn't hear.

- When were you asked to do something you never expected to do—and you did it?

- Who do you listen to?

- What kind of music do you like to dance to?

- Is there something important you've always wanted to do but have never done? What is stopping you?

- Who would you like to get to know better? Why?

Four

"Trust in the Lord with all your heart,
and do not rely on your own insight."

PROVERBS 3:5

You know how
they say:
"It's not
WHAT
you know; It's
WHO
you know that's
so important"?

They're right.

- What are the two or three most stupid things you ever did in your life?

- Who do you trust?

- Think of a time when you *knew* you were in trouble . . . but things worked out instead.

- Who was your favorite teacher? Why?

- Where is your kingdom?

Five

*O Lord, who am I that you should even know
I'm here. And, yet, you have crowned me
with glory and honor.*

FROM PSALM 8

Find a mirror.

Smile.

- Who knows you better than anyone else in the whole world?

- If you could change one thing about yourself, what would it be?

- Relax and look at yourself in the bathroom mirror. *Really* look at yourself: no makeup . . . unshaven . . . no teeth. Now smile. Who do you see?

- What is your name? Who gave it to you? What do you like about it?

- Find as dark a place as possible on a starry night. Look at the stars. Who made you? Who made the stars?

six

I can do anything through God
who gives me strength.

FROM PHILIPPIANS 4:13

"Hold my hand,
Mom,"
the girl whispered
with a quiver in her
little voice.
"OK," her mother said
and took her hand . . .

. . . holding on
to the hope
that she would
always have
Someone
to ask.

- What do you want to do but are afraid to try?

- When was the last time you asked for help?

- Who do you like to hold hands with?

- Think of a time when you *know* you were there for someone else.

- What did the last little voice you listened to say?

Seven

"*With all my heart I praise the Lord,
and with all that I am I praise his holy name!*"

PSALM 103:1, CEV

Do you sing
In the shower?

Why not?

- What song is in your head right now?

- Pretend that you are holding your soul in your hands. What does it look like?

- What is your favorite food to eat on a sunny, summer day?

- What do you look like when you're happy?

- When you're singing alone in the car—and someone sees you—do you sing louder? Or stop altogether?

Eight

"God will wipe every tear from their eyes.
Death will be no more; mourning and crying
and pain will be no more."

REVELATION 21:4

"Remember how we
used to dance?"
he asked.
But she just looked Away.
He wasn't sure
she even knew his name.

He fluffed her pillow
and gently brushed a
silver curl
back off her face.
"It's alright,
my love," he said.
"I remember
Just the same."

- What nicknames do you have? Who uses them?

- Why do we seem to remember so many insignificant things and seem to forget some important ones?

- How did you learn to dance?

- Who do you hope will be by your side when you are very old?

- Who wipes away your tears?

Nine

"There is no longer Jew or Greek,
there is no longer slave or free,
there is no longer male and female;
for all of you are one in Christ Jesus."

GALATIANS 3:28

Who Drew This Line
That
Put
Me
Over
Here
And
You
Over
There
In
The
First
Place?

I WANT NAMES, people!

- When was the last time you saw something happen that was just WRONG? What did you do?

- What lines have *you* drawn that have set you apart from others?

- What has someone done to overcome a division with you?

- Were you usually the first one picked in gym class? Or the last?

- Who creates most of the divisions in your life? Who overcomes them?

Ten

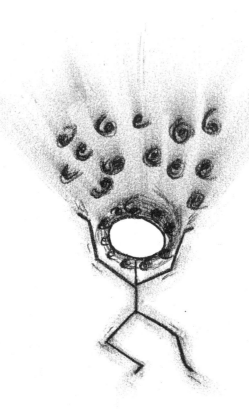

*"In the thirtieth year, in the fourth month,
on the fifth day of the month,
as I was among the exiles by the river Chebar,
the heavens were opened,
and I saw visions of God."*

EZEKIEL 1:1

Dreaming
Is
Wasted

On
Those
Who
Are
Asleep.

- What was the best daydream you ever had?

- What are the most important "dates" on your calendar? Why do they matter so much?

- Think of a time you had to "pinch yourself to see if you were awake" because you couldn't believe something so good was happening.

- Have you ever tried to go back to sleep to finish a dream you were having?

- What desperate situation have you been in that a dream or daydream helped you get through?

Eleven

*There is no distinction. We are all sinners
and fall short of the glory of God.
The truth is: We are saved by God's grace
as a gift, through Jesus Christ.*

FROM ROMANS 3:21-24

"I'd ask you
to come in,"
she said,
"but my house is a
mess."
"Oh,"
she laughed,
"you should see
mine!"

They drank coffee
Together
All afternoon.
And left the dishes
In the sink.

- Which of your friends would your *other* friends not think much of?

- If you could play any game right now, what game would you play?

- Who would you like to spend the afternoon talking to?

- Who has been a friend to you—and you didn't expect them to be?

- When was the last time you received a gift you weren't expecting? Who gave it to you?

Twelve

"You then, my child, be strong in the grace
that is in Christ Jesus;
and what you have learned from me . . ."
TIMOTHY 2:1-2

He tried to get
out the door
without a good-bye
Kiss.
"Get back here,"
she said.
"Mom,
I'm too old for kisses."

"I know I have to
let you go,"
she thought.
"But does it have to
be
today?"

- What "good-bye" in your life has been the hardest?

- When a friend is having a tough time, what do you do?

- What do you *need* to say good-bye to in your life?

- Who gave you your last kiss?

- Who in your life have you learned the most from?

Thirteen

*"For God's foolishness is wiser than
human wisdom,
and God's weakness is stronger than
human strength."*

1 CORINTHIANS 1:25

Things don't always
make sense.

Sometimes
that's a good thing.

- What is the silliest thing you've ever done?

- Who makes you laugh?

- When did what *actually* happen turn out better than what you had planned to have happen?

- Think of the wisest person you know. Describe that person.

- What was the best decision you ever made?

Fourteen

"Answer me when I call
O God of my right!
Remember when you where there for me?
Be gracious to me,
and hear my prayer."

PSALM 4:1

The doctor's words still echoed
in the silence
as they drove home.
"There's something wrong."
She had been so sure
she'd felt
the little guy move.

One hand on the wheel
The other on her belly.
All he could do
was Hope that
they were not alone.

- Is there a hole in your heart? Who cares?

- When have you felt helpless?

- What is the worst news you've ever gotten?

- Do you think anyone hears your prayers?

Fifteen

*When you have eaten your fill
and built your fine houses
and everything you have is multiplied,
do not forget that it is the Lord your God
who has given all these things to you.*

FROM DEUTERONOMY 8:11-20

Let's be honest.

At the end of the day—
And I think you know
what I mean by that—
I will NOT be
Grasping
for my wallet.

- What in your life have you done without anyone else's help?

- Imagine it's fifteen years from now and you're looking back at your life. What will you be most proud of?

- How much of what you have could you give away . . . and still feel like you have more than enough?

- What are you fooling yourself about?

- What was the neighborhood you grew up in like?

sixteen

"Where you go, I will go;
Where you lodge, I will lodge;
Your people shall be my people,
And your God my God."

RUTH 1:16

A fish nibbled
lazily
on the worm
at the end of his line.
Somewhere
a woodpecker
kept time
for the rest of creation.
"Whatcha thinking about?" asked
his friend.
"Nothing much,"
he said.

"Yah, me neither."

- Think back to the third grade. Who was your best friend?

- Where do you think best?

- If you were stranded on a desert island with your family—and one other family—what family would you pick?

- When was the last time you closed your eyes not intending to go to sleep?

- Do you have a quiet place you like to go?

Seventeen

Jacob was alone when the angel came
and they wrestled together all night long.
In the morning, the angel finally said, "Let me go."
But Jacob said, "Not until you bless me."
So the angel did. And Jacob has the limp to prove it.

FROM GENESIS 32:22-32

If you ever see me
Driving in my car
And I look like I'm yelling,
It's probably just me
And God
Having one of our little talks.

It might be a
good idea
to stay out of Our way.

- Who do you know who can yell the loudest?

- When was the last time you had a big fight? Who was it with?

- What really makes you mad?

- What do you do when you know you've been a jerk?

- If you could get an answer to just one question, what question would it be?

Eighteen

Paul told his friends,
"We have this treasure in clay jars,
so that it may be made clear that this extraordinary
power belongs to God and does not come from us."

2 CORINTHIANS 4:7

"Surprise!"
his friends shouted,
proud
that they pulled it off.
And then they sang,
"For he's a jolly
good fellow,"
while he fought back
the tears.
"You shouldn't have,"
was all that he could
Say.

And he meant it.

- Are you easily embarrassed?

- What do you say when someone compliments you?

- Who do you have to thank that you are the person you are?

- Think about the last party you were at.
  What was it for?

- Did you ever think you'd be where you are at this point in your life?

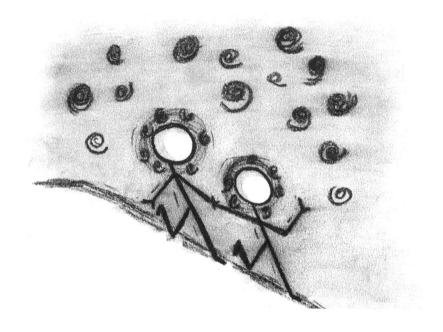

Nineteen

Endure trials for the sake of discipline . . .
now discipline always seems painful
rather than pleasant at the time,
but later it yields the peaceful fruit
of righteousness . . .
Therefore, lift your drooping hands
and strengthen your weak knees
and make straight paths for your feet . . .

FROM HEBREWS 12:7, 11-13

By far the most interesting place
in a river
is the place where
the water
hits the rocks.

That's where the
Movement is
And the rushing
Sound
Of life.

- What was the hardest time in your life? What did you learn from that experience?

- What does your life *sound* like?

- Where is your favorite place to sit and think?

- What changes are taking place in your life right now?

- What makes you keep going strong even when everything seems to be going wrong?

Twenty

*"Do not neglect to show hospitality to strangers,
for by doing that some have entertained angels
without knowing it."*

HEBREWS 13:2

He never said a word,
what could he say?
As he sat there
on the sidewalk
where she passed him
every day.
Her skipping slowed
when she came near.
But her little eyes
contained no fear.
His dirty army jacket
smelled
like something dead:
A dream, too long unfed.

Her daily smile—
I'm not kidding—
was sometimes all
that gave him life.

- Who was once a stranger you didn't like, but is now a friend? How did it happen?

- Do angels have to rest? Or can they just keep flying forever?

- What kills dreams?

- What makes you want to get out of bed in the morning?

- Has anyone ever discouraged one of your good deeds?

Twenty-one

Jesus told Pilate,
"For this I was born, and for this
I came into the world,
to testify to the truth.
Everyone who belongs to the truth
listens to my voice."
And Pilate asked him,
"What is truth?"

JOHN 18:37-38

I used to
Think
I knew it
All.

Pretty funny,
Huh?

- Why are you on this earth? For what were you born?

- Who would you rather get advice from: someone who seems to know everything or the person who admits they don't?

- How can you tell when someone is telling the truth?

- Describe something you always believed to be true but then found out it wasn't.

- Remember when you thought you knew it all? What happened?

Twenty-two

*"God made the wild animals of the earth
of every kind, and the cattle of every kind, and
everything that creeps upon the ground
of every kind. And God saw that it was good."*

GENESIS 1:25

He jumped up beside her
and nuzzled the back of
her neck.
His breath smelled of
Wild things.
His paws were still wet
from the morning dew.
His tail seemed to wag
the whole bed.
He was alive with discovery
And looking forward
To another day.

"How wonderful,"
she thought,
"To smile before I even open my eyes."

- What makes you smile more than anything else?

- How many animals have been a part of your life?

- Are you more like a cat or a dog?

- Do you think you will discover anything *new* today?

- When was the last time you smiled before you opened your eyes? What brought it on?

Twenty-three

*"Who has measured the waters in the
hollow of his hand
and marked off the heavens with a span,
enclosed the dust of the earth in a measure,
and weighed the mountains in scales
and the hills in a balance?
To whom will you liken God . . . ?"*

ISAIAH 40:12, 18

The view from the top
Was
Everything
He imagined it
Would be.
Except for one thing.

Suddenly
He looked
Very small.

- Think back two years ago. What were you reaching for then?

- What is something you find so magnificent you just can't believe it exists?

- What did your dad's hands look like?

- What makes you feel humble?

- What's the best view you ever had? What were you looking at?

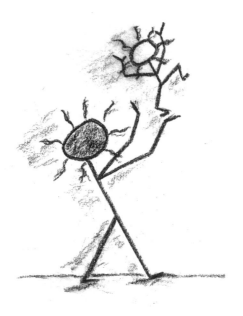

Twenty-four

The really "holy" people couldn't understand:
"Why does Jesus eat with tax collectors and sinners?"
What could he possibly see in them?

FROM MARK 2:15-17

"It's my first car,"
I said.
And he smiled at me.
He knew
what it was like.
"Just don't
slam the doors
too hard,"
he said.
And he was right.
It didn't last long.

But it was mine.

- Where do you look when you pass a homeless person on the street?

- What was your first car? What happened to it?

- Name someone you would *not* like to eat dinner with.

- What do people see when they look at you?

- What are a few of your favorite things?

Twenty-five

"My beloved is all radiant and ruddy,
distinguished among ten thousand.
His head is the finest gold;
his locks are wavy, black as a raven . . .
His lips are lilies . . .
His speech is most sweet . . .
This is my beloved and this is my friend . . ."

SONG OF SOLOMON 5:10-11, 13, 16

"Share my life,"
he said.

"I think I just might
do that,"
I replied.

- Who are you sharing your life with? Why?

- When have you not grabbed hold of an opportunity—and later wished you had?

- What do you think makes a person beautiful?

- Who can you "be yourself" with?

- If you could go back to any one moment in your life, what moment would it be?

Twenty-six

*I pray that you may have the power
to comprehend the breadth and height
and length and depth of all the wonders
God has in store for you!*

FROM EPHESIANS 3:18

The car was packed with coolers and
beach balls and those fold-up chairs
you can sit in right
on the water's edge.
They were all
ready to go.
But it took
an extra hour to find
their youngest son
and persuade him
to come.

He was too busy
Playing in his sandbox
And didn't want to go.

- Look out across the horizon of your life. What are you most looking forward to?

- When was the last time you played in the sand? Or in a puddle? Or in the wet grass?

- What makes you say, "Oh, wow!"

- What is the deepest hole you've ever been in?

- Who is inviting you into some new adventure? Why are you hesitating?

Twenty-seven

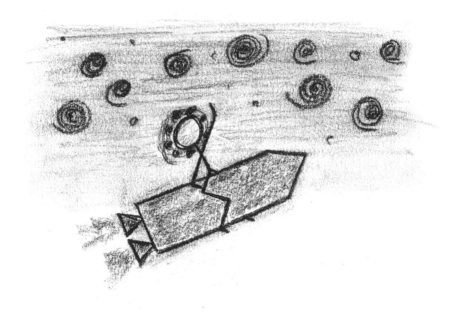

"I am the Alpha and the Omega," says the Lord God,
who is and who was and who is to come,
the Almighty.

REVELATION 1:8

In the future
We'll travel to far off
Places
On ships named
Galaxy Crosser and
We Come in Peace
And we'll mean it.
We'll defy gravity
And all expectations
To the contrary.

But some things
Will never change.

- If you could go anywhere, where would it be?

- Think back eight years ago. What were you doing then that you are still doing today, but you never thought you'd still be doing it?

- Who has been in your life the longest?

- Who is someone you thought was gone forever, but came back?

- What do you think you'll be doing eight years from now?

Twenty-eight

*Jesus said, "Even the hairs of
your head are all counted.
Do not be afraid . . ."*

LUKE 12:7

He sat alone
Looking through a
Window
Watching life
And those who lived it.
The cat purred
And jumped up
On his
Lap.

"Well," he thought,
"she'll miss me
when I'm gone."

- What do you see when you look out your window?

- Who will miss you when you're gone?

- What was the last secret you told? Who did you tell it to?

- Who makes you feel safe?

- What lies ahead that you are afraid of?

Twenty-nine

*Love bears all things, believes all things,
hopes all things, endures all things. . . .
Love never ends.*

FROM 1 CORINTHIANS 13:7-8

Sometimes
It
Will
Hurt.

Love
Anyway.

- What part of you is still hurting right now?

- Do you believe in "happily ever after"?

- Who loves you even though you have hurt them?

- Who was your first love? What happened?

- What is a hurt that was painful, but you can't say you wished it never happened?

Thirty

But God said to him,
"You fool!
This very night
your life is being demanded of you.
And the things you have prepared,
Whose will they be?"

LUKE 12:20

"Did he just say
what I think he said?"
his employees all
wondered
as they packed up
their things
and left early
for the day
"to play."
Yep.
That's what he said.

Three months later
just like
the doctor figured
He was dead.

- If you found out you had three months to live, who would you tell?

- What will people do with your stuff when you're gone?

- When you were little, how *old* did you think grown-ups were?

- When was the last time you just sat around doing nothing?

- Where did your most prized possession come from?

Thirty-one

"I do not understand my own actions.
For I do not do what I want,
but the very thing I hate . . .
I can will what is right, but I cannot do it."

ROMANS 7:15, 18

Thank
Goodness
for
Eve.
God
Knows.

If it wasn't her
It probably would
Have been
Me.

- Think of something you did wrong. Did you know it was wrong before you did it?

- What is a temptation you just can't seem to stay away from?

- What are you most sorry for?

- Have you ever set someone up to be tempted or to get in trouble?

- Imagine you're sitting under a tree all by yourself. What are you thinking about?

Thirty-two

"*What does the Lord require of you but to
do justice, and to love kindness,
and to walk humbly with your God?*"

MICAH 6:8

Most of the
things
that we think
matter . . .

Don't.

- What is the most important thing you have ever done?

- Who is the most humble person you know?

- Have you ever thought about what you'd like your tombstone to say?

- When you walk into a room, can you tell who the "important" people are? How?

- When you were seven years old, what did you want to be when you grew up?

Thirty-three

"Seek the Lord while he may be found,
call upon him while he is near;
let the wicked forsake their way,
and the unrighteous their thoughts;
let them return to the Lord,
that he may have mercy on them,
and to our God,
for he will abundantly pardon."

ISAIAH 55:6-7

She carried her
secret past
around like a weapon.
No one else knew
the dark places
she had been.
They just thought
she was awful crabby
and always
Alone.

I bet if she had just said, "I'm sorry,"
she would have made
some friends.

- When was the last time you said, "I'm sorry"?

- Where does the light go when it gets dark?

- What weapons do you use to keep people from getting too close to you?

- Who are you pushing away right now?

- What one thing are you afraid someone might find out about you?

Thirty-four

*"Even though I walk
through the darkest valley,
I fear no evil;
for you are with me."*

PSALM 23:4

You are crying
Into my shoulder
Breaking my heart
With every sob.
No Band-Aid,
No tender kiss,
No purple Popsicle
Can take away your
Very
Grown-up pain.

But, maybe,
if I hold you tight enough, together,
we can live to see
another day.

- What is the darkest time in your life?

- Who has seen you cry?

- What does evil look like?

- Think back seven years—what did you fear then?

- What do you do when you can't help someone's pain go away?

Thirty-five

The man came back to thank Jesus
for healing him.
But Jesus said,
"Get up and go on your way;
your faith has made you well."

FROM LUKE 17:19

Something
Miraculous
Happened
Today.

Did you see it?

- If a miracle happens with no one to see it—
  does it still take place?

- Can people make miracles happen?

- Who believes in you?

- Look around you. Right now.
  What is the most amazing thing you see?

- How does a television work?

Thirty-six

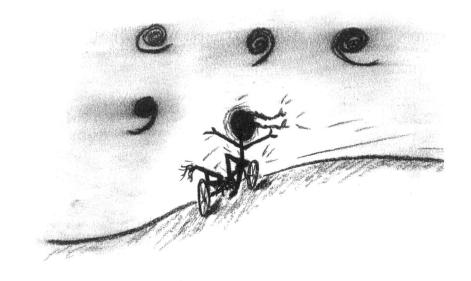

Jesus said to his friends,
"Remember,
I am always with you,
to the end of time."

FROM MATTHEW 28:20

He took the first
flight
he could get
and was there
within hours.
All the memories
of ancient battles,
pulled pigtails,
teasing words
Forgotten.
His sister needed him.
and he was there.

She was only sorry
she waited so long
to ask.

- When was the last time you rode a bike with no hands?

- Who is your oldest friend?

- If you were really sick, who would you call?

- Is there somebody in your family you wish you could see right now?

- What would it take for you to go see your worst enemy?

Thirty-seven

"Let us consider how to provoke
one another
to love and good deeds."

HEBREWS 10:24

Hey, you . . .

What have you done
For somebody else
Lately?

- Whose life have you changed?

- Why are some people so nice? And some so mean?

- When was the last time you were on a swing?
  Was someone pushing you?

- Do you make eye contact with strangers?

- What did you do or say today that you didn't have
  to and it made someone smile?

Thirty-eight

". . . the promise is for you,
for your children,
and for all who are far away . . ."

ACTS 2:39

The street was fairly quiet
on these early
morning walks.
There were joggers
and other dog-walkers
and early-shift workers
making their way
with sleepy determination.
His dog pulled at the leash
as if to say, "Let's go."
But he would not be
Hurried.

He saw it as his personal
mission
to greet everyone he saw
and say, "Hello."

- What out-of-the-ordinary thing made your day today?

- When was the last time you said hello to someone you didn't know, just for fun?

- What promise did you make at least five years ago that you have never broken?

- When you're in an elevator, do you make eye contact with the other people on it?

- Where is your favorite place to walk?

Thirty-nine

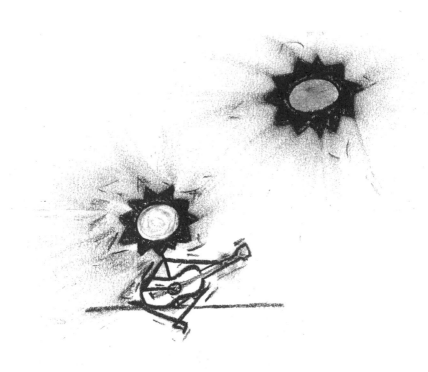

"Don't let me be too poor or too rich . . .
If I have too much to eat, I might forget about you;
if I don't have enough I might steal and
disgrace your name."

PROVERBS 30:7-9, CEV

I remember
hearing someone say
that all they wanted
was to make a
Decent Living.

What do you think
they meant
by that?

- Who is the richest person you know?

- What does a child truly need to have a decent living?

- If you had more time, what would you do with it?

- What is the biggest challenge a poor person faces? How about a wealthy one?

- What do you have now that you never thought you'd have? Is it everything you hoped it would be? Could you live without it?

Forty

"Right away the rooster crowed a second time.
Then Peter remembered that Jesus had told him,
'Before a rooster crows twice, you will say
three times that you don't know me.'
So Peter started crying."

MARK 14:72

Tears ran down
the old man's cheeks.
The nurse said,
"Don't stay long."
After everything
he'd said and done
—even now—
he didn't think
his boy would come.
"I'm sorry, Son,"
he finally said.

"I Know that, Dad."
Besides, it was a
long time ago.

- What act of kindness have you never forgotten?

- Who do you need to say you're sorry to?

- Describe the house you were born in.

- Think about a time when you looked the other way and later regretted it.

- When was the last time you cried?

Forty-one

Moses couldn't believe his eyes.
The bush was blazing, but it was not burned up.
Then Moses heard God calling, "Moses, Moses!"
And Moses said, "Here I am."
Then God said, "Come no closer!
Remove the sandals from your feet,
for the place on which you are standing is
holy ground."

FROM EXODUS 3:1-5

The children parted
like the sea
when she rolled in.
A little girl
with legs that
couldn't run
or dance
or hang upside down
from monkey bars
on a sunny day.
And they were scared.
They stared.

And then one said,
"Hi.
Come sit next to me."

- Who makes you feel uncomfortable?

- You have a weakness most people don't see. What is it?

- What is the most special place you've ever been?

- Think of a time you were a leader. Describe it.

- What is your favorite pair of shoes?

Forty-two

"*Listen, I will tell you a mystery!*
We will not all die, but we will all be changed,
in a moment, in the twinkling of an eye,
at the last trumpet . . ."

1 CORINTHIANS 15:51-52

She held the yellowed
photograph
in her wrinkled
hand.

"I never knew how
beautiful
I was," she said.

- Think of a person you cared about who has died. How did that person make a difference in your life?

- Think back exactly fourteen years. What were you thinking about then?

- If you could take three things with you to heaven (people not included) what would you take?

- What causes change in you?

- What do you want to be doing when the trumpet sounds for you?

Forty-three

Jesus said to them,
"I am the bread of life.
Whoever comes to me
will never be hungry,
and whoever believes in me
will never be thirsty."

JOHN 6:35

The sign said "walk"
but he stood still
as the mob rushed off to 30th floor
offices and other
very
important
places.
The tie around his neck
felt unusually tight.

"Are you alright?"
a woman asked him.
But he didn't know what
to say.

- Is there somewhere important you're supposed to be?

- Who has shown you kindness out of the blue?

- Where do you fit "in the big picture"?

- Have you ever felt so trapped you couldn't breathe?

- What is the hungriest you have ever been?

Forty-four

There is a power at work within us
—you know Who it is—
through which we can accomplish
abundantly far more
than anything we could ask
or even imagine.

FROM EPHESIANS 3:20

Did you ever do
Something
So remarkably kind
Or courageous
That you thought to yourself,

"That couldn't possibly
have been
me."

- When was the last time you patted yourself on the back?

- Who are you most like: the Scarecrow, the Tin Man, or the Cowardly Lion?

- What is the most courageous thing you have ever done?

- What do you like to think you see when you look in a mirror?

- Have you ever felt a "power" at work in you? How do you explain it?

Forty-five

Lord, you have searched me and known me.
You know when I sit down and when I rise up;
you discern my thoughts from far away.
You search out my path and my lying down,
and are acquainted with all my ways.
You hem me in, behind and before,
and lay your hand upon me."

PSALM 139:1-3, 5

His luggage was lost
Again.
He had watched
The bags
That were not his
Go round
And round.
He had a meeting
In the morning.

He hoped by then
he'd remember what
town
he was in.

- Have you ever forgotten where you were?

- Who do you go to for direction in your life?

- What keeps happening to you over and over that you wish you could stop?

- Where do you want to be headed?

- What in your life helps keep you on track?

Forty-six

Jesus said, "Blessed are the merciful,
for they will receive mercy. . . .
Blessed are the peacemakers, for they will be called
children of God."

MATTHEW 5:7, 9

I
Can
Hold
A
Grudge
For
A
Very
Long
Time.

Or not.

- Think of someone who has every right to be really, really mad—but isn't.

- You know that dark place inside you? What's in there?

- Who has wronged you?

- Remember when you were a kid and you used to run around in the rain? Can you remember the cool, clean water running down your face? Can you remember laughing?

- Look around you. Who looks unhappy?

Forty-seven

"God called the dry land Earth,
and the waters that were gathered together
God called Seas.
And God saw that it was good."

GENESIS 1:10

The lawn mower roared
to a stop.
She looked out
across
the blanket of green
grass
now neatly trimmed
and standing proudly
at attention—

She loved tending to
Her little corner
Of creation.

- What part of your world would run out of control if not for your care and attention?

- What have you created?

- When did you last stop to pick some flowers on the side of the road?

- Where is your favorite place in the world?

- Do you have a favorite chore? Why do you enjoy doing it?

Forty-eight

*Mary and the other women ran
to tell the disciples that
Jesus had been raised.
But their words seemed so foolish and
their tale so ridiculous
that they did not believe them.*

FROM LUKE 24:1-24

"Papa,"
the little boy said, Tugging on
his grandpa's sleeve.
"Don't cry.
Nana's in heaven
with the angels
now."

But later that night
the little guy
cried himself
to sleep.

- Have you ever cried yourself to sleep?

- Who do you miss more than anyone?

- What was your grandma like?

- Describe heaven. Or draw it.

- If you could meet an angel, what would you say?

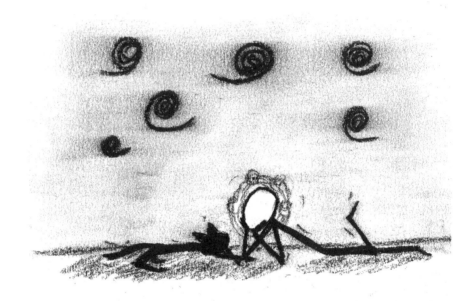

Forty-nine

Jesus said,
"Come to me, all you that are weary
and are carrying heavy burdens,
and I will give you rest."

MATTHEW 11:28

He buried his face in her fur.
He could hear the purr that said,
"I can't imagine life
without you."

In all his life,
he thought,
He'd never find
A friend
More faithful.

- Did you have a favorite stuffed animal when you were a kid?

- Who are you faithful to?

- Have you ever purred?

- Who can you not imagine being without?

- What kind of animal do you prefer for a pet?

Fifty

Stop worrying!
Seek first the kingdom of God
and everything else you need
will be yours.

FROM LUKE 12:29-31

Where is it
Written
That you can
Only
Have
So
Much
Fun?

Nowhere.
That's where.

- Think back thirteen years ago. What did you do for fun then?

- What are you worrying about right now?

- If you could sail away, who would you want to go with you? What would you be sailing away from?

- When was the last time someone did something for you that you didn't expect at all? What was it?

- What are you looking for these days?

Fifty-one

Jesus woke up and told the wind to stop.
Then he said to the sea, "Peace! Be still!"
And the wind stopped. And the sea was calm.
And, just like that, the storm was over.
He looked at his disciples and said,
"Just WHAT exactly were you so afraid of?"

FROM MARK 4:35-41

He came in
as soon as the thunder
rolled in.
"Aren't you afraid?"
he whispered
to the little lump
snuggled quietly
under the covers.

"Don't be silly, Daddy,"
the sleepy voice said.
"But could you
sing to me
before you leave?"

- What little, snugly lumps do you care about?

- When are your scariest moments?

- Who was the last person you sang to? Told a joke to? Said, "I love you" to?

- Who is your favorite superhero? Why?

- Who do you depend on for comfort in hard and scary times?

Fifty-two

Jesus told them another parable:
"The kingdom of heaven is like yeast
that a woman took and mixed in
with three measures of flour
until all of it was leavened."

MATTHEW 13:33

Do you really
Think
That what you do
Doesn't
Make
A
Difference?

Tell me,
Where do you come
UP
With this stuff?!?

- What is a small thing that you did that wound up having a big impact?

- What does the smell of freshly baked bread remind you of?

- Where are you making a difference? Who knows about it?

- Who is someone who did something small that made a huge difference in your life? Did you thank them?

- What's the dumbest thing anybody ever told you?

A word of thanks

It takes a lot of people to make any book happen. And we probably needed more help and encouragement than most! Thanks to all the folks at Augsburg Fortress who are trying courageously to move in new directions. You guys "get it"!

Thanks, too, to the good people at Cross of Glory who put up with random acts of creativity and the occasional chaos that accompanies it; you are making a difference in the church and in the world.

Thanks to our families—especially Emma and Ethan (who are the best thing, with God's help, we have ever created)—and friends too many to name who take us seriously in spite of ourselves. You know us . . . and love us anyway!

Thanks to everybody who read this book and convinced us that we weren't crazy, especially Pete (thanks for that late night December lecture) & Steph; Rudy & Jinny & Paul & Allison (who let us share this silly idea over the best Thanksgiving turkey ever); Lori (for more than you know) & Dwayne (the "holy-moley" man); and you

Mom . . . the tears you shed at our kitchen table even after laughing at these silly "stick people" convinced us we were on to something. Thanks for always cheering us on.

And, finally, we don't even know HOW to say thanks to Andrew, who would figure out a way to "beam us up" if we asked him, and to Tana, who always keeps the glass at least half full. We love you guys. And we couldn't do what we do without you.

—*Kelly & Tim*

About the authors

Kelly A. Fryer is the author of *No Experience Necessary: On the Job Training for a Life of Faith* (Augsburg Fortress, 1999) and pastor at Cross of Glory Lutheran Church in Lockport, Illinois. Timothy J. Ressmeyer, Ph.D., is a social scientist and vice president at a Chicago-based market research firm. Kelly and Tim met in a political-science class at Valparaiso University. They have been married for nineteen years, have two children (Emma and Ethan), two dogs (Teddy and Roosevelt), and one cat (Franklin).